Ross Moore Stokes Family Ties

Bonita Stokes Walker

Compiled by family members

DEDICATION

This book is dedicated to all the descendants of Joe Moore and Mary Tyler so that our future generations can get a beginning sketch of our ancestors and all of our connections.

CONTENTS

Acknowledgments   i

Introduction   Pg. 1

1 The Moore Family   Pg. 2

2 The Stokes and Moore Family Meet Pg. 5

3 John D. Barron   Pg. 8

4 Raleigh Lee Stokes   Pg. 11

5 Andrew Stokes   Pg. 15

6 Ernest Stokes   Pg. 17

7 Chalmers Stokes   Pg. 26

8 Clarence and James Stokes   Pg. 27

9 Marcellus Stokes   Pg. 29

10 Marcellars Moore Jr.   Pg. 34

11 Raleigh Moore   Pg. 40

More Family Photos   Pg. 41

Census Records   Pg. 43

ACKNOWLEDGMENTS

I would like to thank those family members who submitted pictures and biographical information willingly and early so we could have some idea of the vast spread of our family. I want to say a special thanks to Rita and M.C. Moore for allowing me to pick their brains about many of the family members who were unable to respond to my call for information.

INTRODUCTION

"When an older person dies, it's like a library burned. Once they go, they take everything with them." This quote is often attributed to Alex Haley. But I found that this is an old African griot saying.

I have gathered these pictures and brief bios of family members because it is so important to tell our stories as we live it. Our future generations will depend upon it. Our ancestors' history has only been partially uncovered. Most of it is due to slavery. But a large part is because our history isn't written. While even an oral history is great to have, it has its flaws. Stories change over the years as they are retold. Far too many stories have been left untold.

According to genealogist Thomas Burroughs, in the old countries, Gambia, Sierra Leone, Nigeria, etc. there were griots who kept a great deal of information that they could recite on request. Griots could recount the history of a village for 125 years or more. The farther back in history they would cite, less information was told about the average villager and more information was told about the leaders and chiefs. So the average villager could still only receive a brief account of his or her family history.

Today, we do not have griots telling our stories. As our older generations die out, their stories are told less frequently and with a lot less accuracy. All the more reason to record the stories as we make them and to uncover those stories that we can.

1
THE MOORE FAMILY

Mary Jane Tyler, daughter of Derill and Martha Tyler, was born around 1845 in Yalobusha, Misssissippi. She was 15 years old at the time the 1860 census was taken and one of seven siblings. At some point in the late 1800s, **Joe Moore** married Mary Jane Tyler, and as someone jokingly said at an earlier reunion, making her the original Mary Tyler Moore. They had 14 children, but only four lived – Marcellus (1868-19??), Raleigh (1883-1966), Walter (1894 – 19??), also known as Dump, and Isaiah (1896 – 19??). Unfortunately, I have no information on Isaiah or Walter. Marcellus's and Raleigh's descendants are listed briefly below and in more detail later along with information about their spouses. As of this printing, I've uncovered no pictures of either Joe Moore or Mary Tyler Moore.

JOE MOORE AND MARY TYLER

Children	Grandchildren	Gr Grandchildren Gr Gr Grandchildren
1. Marcellars Moore (1868 – 19??)	Adelina Moore *	John (J.D.) Barron
		Luberda Barron
		Dora Mae Barron
		Pearline Barron
		James Edward Barron
		Letha Ann Barron
		Emma Jean Barron
		Raleigh Stokes
		James "J.C." Stokes
		Dorothy Mae Stokes
		James Stokes Charles Blue

Clarence Stokes Sr.
> Clarence Stokes Jr.
> Clara Stokes
> Calvin Stokes
> Bertha Lee Stokes
> Mary Joyce Stokes

Ernest Stokes
> Ervin Cornelius Stokes
> Bonita Rachel Stokes
> Sharon Louise Stokes
> Ernest Stokes
> Elona Moore
> Sevare Stokes
> Sherman Laray Stokes
> Charmaine Louise Stokes
> Victor Kevin Stokes

Andrew Stokes
> Cynthia Stokes

Chalmers Stokes
> Frank Poole
> Shari Stokes
> Charles Stokes
> Mary Helen Stokes

Marcellus Stokes Sr.
> Marcellus "Mark" Stokes Jr.
> Robert Anthony Stokes Sr.
> Brenda Stokes
> Ronald Stokes
> Kenneth William Stokes Sr.
> Ilene Marie Stokes
> Valerie Jewel Stokes
> James Daniel Stokes

Marcellars Moore Jr.

Celeste Moore

Anna Moore
> Sonia Moore
> George Bingham Jr.

Mattie Moore
> Clydee Bell Atkins
> Arnold Gene Atkins
> Alfred Atkins
> Pamela Atkins
> David Atkins

Colleen Marie Moore
> Frank Stamps

David Moore (no children)

Marcellars "M.C." Moore
> Gwendolyn Moore
> Sharon Jackson

Marcellars "M.C." Moore cont . . .
　　Darren Moore
　　Tina Moore
　　Byron Moore
　　Charlotte Moore
　　Annette Moore
　　Yvette Baxter
　　Yolanda Baxter
　　Donna Baxter
Frederick Moore Sr.
　　Frederick Moore Jr.
　　Larry MacIntosh
　　Diane Perry
　　Shirley McFerren

Altha Moore (no children)

2. Raliegh Moore   Edward "E.C." Moore   David Moore
　(1883 – 1966)   Leslie Moore
　　　　　　　　　　　　　　　　　　　　　　Linda Moore

Theary Moore Sr.   Theary Moore Jr.
　　　　　　　　　　　　　　　　　Linda Moore

Orange W. Moore   Orlanda Moore
　　　　　　　　　　　　　　　Sandra Moore

Raleigh "R.L." Moore   (no children)
Overzina Moore **   Ronald Ross
　　　　　　　　　　　　　　Lorraine Ross
　　　　　　　　　　　　　　Paul Ross
　　　　　　　　　　　　　　　　Tori Ross
　　　　　　　　　　　　　　　　Joey Ross
　　　　　　　　　　　　　　　　Michael Ross
　　　　　　　　　　　　　　Barbara Ross
　　　　　　　　　　　　　　　　Kelly Orange
　　　　　　　　　　　　　　Jesse Ross
　　　　　　　　　　　　　　James Ross

3. Walter Moore   *(no further information available at this time)*
　(1894 – 19??)
4. Isaiah Moore   *(no further information available at this time)*
　(1896 – 19??)

*   It was Adelina Moore who married Daniel Stokes to bring the Stokes line into our family.

**   It was Overzina Moore who married Lorenzo Ross to bring the Ross line into our family.

2

THE STOKES AND MOORE FAMLIES MEET

| Marcellars Moore (1868 – 19??) son of Joe Moore and Mary Tyler | Marcellars Moore (same as left, taken earlier) | Mary Ella (maiden name unknown) |

The family name Stokes can be found on the census records dating back to 1790 with Henry Stokes as the head of the family and his wife, Rioriah (spelling is partially illegible on census). Together they had 12 children, including John Stokes. John married Nellie Wilson. Together they also had 12 children. All of their children were born in rural Mississippi. Among them was a son named Daniel S. Stokes. The Stokes family was neighbors to the Moore family during the early 1900s. Based on what is on the census record, one can only speculate what happened. The 1910 Census shows Marcellus (b. 1868) (spelled Marcellars) Moore as head of house hold. He was married to Ella whom is also known as Mary Ella pictured above. Present day family refer to her as "Grandma Mary." Together, they had five children, only three survived – Adelina, Marcellars (b.1897) and Altha. The Marcellars born in 1897 is M.C.'s (b. 1930) father. The same M.C. who currently lives in St. Louis, Missouri with his wife, Rita.

At the time of the 1910 Census, it shows that Adelina (also spelled Atleana) was married to a man by the name of Marion Walton, and that they had one child who was listed as living at the time the census record was taken. That child's name, however, does not appear on the census in their household. Since census workers were highly underpaid, inexperienced record keepers, anything could be the reason the child's name does not show up as a member of this household. It could be an oversight on the part of the family or the census worker or perhaps even both. It could also be that the child had been given away to another family member or friend to be cared for as Adelina was only 17 years old when the census was taken. Since it said she had been married for two years, it seems unlikely that the child would have been given away. Otherwise, why marry? If the child had died, then the census should have told the story that the child was no longer living. Omission of the child's name remains an unsolved mystery in the family tree.

In any event, the marriage between Adelina and Marion did not last. Again only speculation here: were they divorced, did he die? It would be interesting to dig up that piece of history and document it. What we do know is that at some point, Daniel S. Stokes from down the street, came calling and eventually married Adelina.

The 1910 Census also shows that Daniel was a widower. While we don't have any information about his previous marriage, we do know of a previous relationship which resulted in the birth of his first son, John Daniel Barron. Rumor has it that Daniel, who was married at the time, was a school teacher and began a relationship with a 13 year old student named Dolly Hunt. Dolly eventually became pregnant, and because of the scandalous nature of such a young girl being with child, Dolly's mother agreed on her marrying a family friend and minister, Robert Barren. The child was named John D. Barron, with Minister Barron shown as the father of record. Robert and Dolly later had additional children. J.D. grew up not knowing that Robert wasn't his biological father. He was an adult when he found out that Daniel was his father.

Daniel, however, was well aware that the child, J. D. as he came to be called, was his son. So after Daniel and Adelina married, the two families, the Barrons and the Stokes continued a long lasting familial relationship. The Stokes clan led by Daniel began their family in Mississippi. They had children born in both Crowder and Lambert, Mississippi. The Stokes family was known for lots of offspring. There were 12 siblings among Daniel's family and 12 siblings among Daniel's father's family. The union between Daniel and Adelina brought six sons and one daughter into the fold. Adding in J.D., there were seven boys and one girl all together. The girl whose name I have yet to uncover died at an early age. So the Stokes brothers as we know them today include:

> John D. Barren, aka J.D. (2 Oct. 1909 – 8 Dec. 1989)
>
> Raleigh Lee "R.L." Stokes (1914 – 19??)
>
> Andrew Stokes (16 May 1918 – 9 Feb. 1988)
>
> James Stokes
>
> Clarence William Stokes, Sr. (19?? - 1973)
>
> Ernest Severe Stokes aka Sevare Ernest Stokes (18 Aug. 1923 – 7 Mar. 1992)
>
> Chalmers Stokes (4 Dec. 1925 – 15 Aug. 1973)
>
> Marcellus Stokes aka "Red Boy" (23 Mar. 1928 – 23 Feb. 2009)

Daniel Stokes

Adelina Stokes

The picture on the right had the name Daniel written on the back of it. As far as the family knows, Adelina did not have a child named Daniel. One theory as to who the baby might be is R.L., their first child together. Someone just wrote the name Daniel to indicate that the picture is of Daniel's family.

3
JOHN D. BARRON

JOHN DANIEL BARRON, SPOUSE MARY JOHNSON
(2 OCT. 1909 – 8 DEC. 1989)

1. Luberda Barron
     (21 Feb. 1931 – 29 May 2013)
     -m- Henderson Howard, a factory
        worker and barber

Georgia Louise Barren
(10 Aug. 1950 –)
Betty Jean Barren
(30 Oct. 1951 –)
Linda Howard
(14 May 1955 –)
Tyrone Howard
(22 May 1956 –)
Vince Howard
(23 Apr. 1957 –)
Deniece Howard
(21 Feb. 1960 –)
Mary Howard
(19 Dec. 1961 –)
Darnell Howard
(11 Aug. 1966 –)
Lonnell Howard
(11 Aug. 1966 –)

2. Dora Mae Barron
    (9 Jan. 1933 – 8 July 1996)
    -m- Cassie Love Sr., a railroad worker
        who had one of the most
        beautiful gardens in town

Cassie Love Jr.
Dorothy Mae Love
Fatina Love
Geraldine Love
Marvin Love
Zachary Love
Doris Mae Love
(12 Apr. 1950 –)
Edward Love
(22 May 1952 – July 2007)
Donnie Love
(17 Nov. 1953 –)

3. Pearline Barron
   (3 Aug. 1935 – 7 Feb. 1989)
   -m- Johnny Johnson, a school teacher

   As her name implies, Pearline
   was often referred to as a
   precious jewel because she was
   so nice.

Belinda Love
(18 June 1955 –)
Harvey Love
(7 Oct. 1957 –)
Harry Johnson
(20 June 1955 –)
Larry Johnson
(20 June 1955 –)
Jackie Johnson
(5 Feb. 1957 –)
Johnny Ray Johnson
(20 Jan. 1958 – 19 Feb. 1984)
Douglas Johnson
(1 July about 1960 –)

4. James Edward Barron
   (2 Oct. 1943 – 8 Jan. 2001)

5. Letha Ann Barron "Sister"
   (2 Mar. 1947 –)
   -m-   Buckley

Cory Larnell Buckley
(11 Sep. 1972 –)
Laotis Darnell Buckley
(3 Dec. 1974 –)
Jabrina Janell Buckley
(5 Aug. 1978 –)

6. Emma Jean Barron
   (18 Feb. 1952 –)

Sally K. Henderson
(30 Dec. 1975 –)
-m- James Carter

Jazzlyn Carter
(7 July 1996 –)
James Carter
(12 Aug. 2000 –)
Jalyce Carter
(2 Sep. 2001 –)

Cornicha Rochelle Henderson
(2 Feb. 1977 –)
-m- Brian West

Brianna West
(30 Mar. 2000 –)
Mia West
(13 July 2006 –)
Brian West Jr.

Monique Nicole Riley
(3 July 1982 –)
-m- James Pierre

Jalen Pierre
(7 June 2002 –)
Jalaya Pierre
(6 July 2004 –)
Jaianna Pierre
(15 Sep. 2008 –)

Emma Barron and Brianna West

Brian Sr., Brianna, Cornicha, Brian Jr., Mia

4
RALEIGH LEE STOKES

RALEIGH LEE STOKES, SPOUSE ANNIE LEE STOKES
(about 1914 – 19??)

Children	**Grandchildren**	**Great Grandchildren** **Gr-Gr Grandchildren**
James "J.C." Stokes	Lakrisca Stokes (12 Nov. ?? –) -m- Sydney C. Gaut	Lauren Gaut Kathleen Gaut

Lakrisca and Sydney Gaut

Lauren and Lakrisca ready for Lauren's
eighth grade promotion ceremony

Children	Grandchildren	Great Grandchildren Great Great Grandchildren
Dorothy Mae Stokes (24 Jan. 1932 –) -m- Earl Patton Ruffin Sr. (deceased) -m- Ivory Watkins (deceased)	1. Theresa Stokes (2 Apr. 1950 –) -m- Jonathan Michael Parker (7 Mar. 19?? – 8 May 1998) 2. Patricia Ann Stokes (8 Mar. 1951 –) -m- Timothy White (5 Oct. 1959 –)	
	3. Theodore Ruffin (17 Jan. 1952 –) -m- Althea Washington (5 Mar. 1960 –)	LaShaunda Monique Ruffin (2 Jan. 1987 –) -m- Melvin Woods
	4. Earl Patton Ruffin Jr. (23 Sep. 1955 – 17 Apr. 2011) -m- Debra Stokes (22 Nov. 1953 –) 5. Lonnie Darnell Ruffin (16 Sep. 1957 – Jan. 1998) -m- Cynthia D. Thomas	Earl Cumming DeAngelo Cumming
	6. Glenda Ruffin (9 Dec. 1960 –) -m- Dennis Orlando Williams (10 July 1956 – 21 Oct. 1986)	Kenyetta Tamika Monique Ruffin (23 Jan. 1976 –) Darrell Eschon Orlando Franklin (25 June 1992 –) Reginald Franklin Jr. (22 Oct. 1994 –) Raymond Jamal Patillo (12 Apr. 1996 –) Alicia Tamia Monique Kirschke (17 May 2000 –) Latifha Maxine Perry (9 June 1990 –) Harmonie Mircal Brown (18 Sep. 2010 –)

Earl Patton Ruffin Jr. married his sweetheart, Debra Stokes, who is apparently no kin to this Stokes family, on October 18, 2003. They enjoyed almost eight years of married life together before Earl was called home to Glory.

Dorothy Mae Stokes Watkins says, "I have lived a good life. The Lord let me see my children become adults, to see my grandchildren, and their children. I praise Him for that. Thank you, Lord!"

Glenda Williams

Kenyetta Ruffin

Latifha Perry

Reginald Franklin

Darrell Franklin

Raymond Patillo

Alicia Kirschke

Harmonie Brown

Theodore Ruffin

Althea Ruffin

5
ANDREW STOKES

ANDREW STOKES, SPOUSE – ETHEL MAE BURCH
(16 MAY 1918 – 9 FEB. 1988)

Children

Cynthia Stokes
(14 May 1956 –)
-m- John Hardyway Sr.
 (1 Apr. 1954)

Grandchildren

John Hardyway Jr.
(9 Feb. 1978 –)
 -m- Veronika
        Araszkiewicz
(4 Feb. 1981 –)

Joseph Alan Hardyway
(6 Mar. 1981 –)

John Jr. and Veronika Hardyway

Cynthia Hardyway

John Hardyway Jr. graduated with two masters degrees from Wayne State University in 2013. One was in Anthropology and the other was in Geology.

Cynthia, John Jr., and John Hardyway Sr.

Cynthia Hardyway cont….

Christopher Lee Hardyway
(29 May 1982 –)
-m- Ny'Ree Sisk
(20 Apr. 1980 –)

Christopher Emmanuel Hardyway
(27 Sep. 2004 –)
Nyris Amari Hardyway
(1 Mar. 2007 –)
Miren Monique Hardyway
(7 Jan. 2011 –)

Jayson Hardyway
(15 June 1984 –)

Courtney Hardyway
(17 Aug. 1988 –)

Father is Isaiah Prince Owens
Liam Andrew Owens
(18 June 2014 –)

Courtney Hardyway

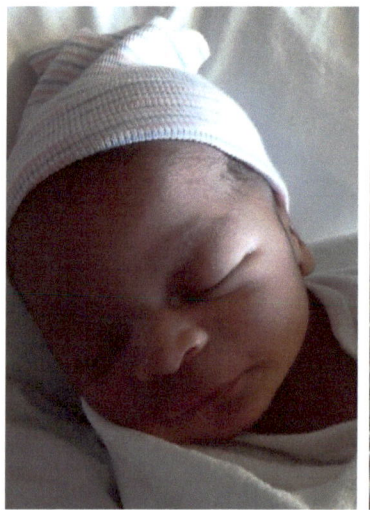

Liam Andrew Owens

Nyris, Miren, and Chris Hardyway

Ny'Ree Hardyway

6
ERNEST SEVARE STOKES

ERNEST SEVARE STOKES, SPOUSE – ROSA BEA LOCKS
(18 Aug. 1923 – 7 Mar. 1992)   (16 Mar. 1929 – 14 Aug. 1977)

Children	Grandchildren	Great Grandchildren
1. Ervin Cornelius Stokes (17 Feb. 1951 – 11 July 2011) -m- Wannetta Page (div) (25 Nov. 1953 –)	Shannon Cornelius (23 May 1974 –) -m- Dea Hatcher Shauneta Catrice Stokes (20 May, 1980 –)	Isiah Cornelius Stokes (4 Apr. 2008 –)

Ervin Cornelius Stokes

Dea and Isiah Stokes

Ervin Stokes enjoyed entertaining children with his puppet ministry. He showed his love for friends and family by sending virtually everyone he knew a birthday card each year along with a scripture and a joke.

Dea and Shannon Stokes

Isiah Stokes

Shauneta Catrice Stokes

Children	**Grandchildren**	**Great Grandchildren**
2. Bonita Rachel Stokes (20 May 1953 –)	Yvetta Rachelle Stokes (13 Oct. 1969 –)	
	Jamila Michelle Walker (5 Nov. 1983 –)	Preston Kyle Walker (14 Oct. 2005 –)

Bonita Rachel Walker

Yvetta Washington and Jamila Walker

Bonita Walker retired from her career as an elementary school teacher in June 2013. Prior to her teaching career, she worked in the telecommunications industry for 16 years while earning her Bachelor's degree in Journalism and her Master's degree in Elementary Education from Wayne State University. She enjoys genealogy research, writing, and traveling. An entrepreneur at heart, Bonita currently is a network marketer in the travel industry.

Preston and Jamila Walker

Preston

19

3. Sharon Louise Stokes
   (20 Oct. 1959 –)

Sharon Stokes retired from the army after serving 25 years. She currently works for the United States government. She spends her spare time traveling and promoting her network marketing travel business.

ERNEST STOKES, SPOUSE – GERALDINE MALLORY

4. Sevare Samuel Stokes   Severe Samuel Stokes Sr.   Severe Samuel Stokes Jr.
   (13 Aug. 1961 –)
   -m- Carline Stokes
   (25 June 19?? –)

Sevare, Severe Jr., and Severe Sr.

5. Sherman Laray Stokes
   (12 Aug. 1962 –)
   -m- Alice Melonee Stokes
   (7 Apr. 1949 –)

Kevin Brian Collins, *son of Alice*

Mother is Renee Hunter
Reaunna Shartavia Hunter
   (5 Feb. 1993 –)
Anthony Hunter

Deannah Brownleaf

Aamire Hunter

Sherman Stokes was born in Detroit, but was raised most of his life in St. Louis, Missouri. Swimming has always been his claim to fame as a competitor and a coach. He retired from the City of Detroit after 30 years of service where he worked in the Department of Recreation and Police Department.

"God has been a blessing to me to enjoy my three children, two grandchildren, and loving wife of 15 years."

Alice and Sherman

Reaunna and Allice

Anthony, Reaunna, and Charmaine

5. Charmaine Louise Stokes
  (12 Aug. 1962 –)

Zynquwandria Sonovia Stokes
  (7 Mar. 1980 –)

Nathaniel Stokes
  (8 Nov. 1999 –)

Luquinda Shynda Stokes
  (17 May 1981 –)

Charquita Latoya Stokes
  (9 May 1982 –)

Sharneise Stokes
  (26 Aug. 1996 –)
Tre'Veon Stokes
  (13 May 2001 –)
Donald Cathey
  (16 Aug. 2005 –)
Chardanae Cathey
  (7 July 2006 –)
Dennis Cathey
  (11 June 2007 –)
Storee Cathey
  (28 Nov. 2012 –)

Dale Dajuan Stokes
  (3 Apr. 1983 –)
engaged to Jardale Wilson
  (19 June 1982 –)

Raijanee Powell
Dale Damoney Stokes
Dalegotti DaRich Stokes
  (20 Dec. 2012 –)

Jerrell Shannon Stokes
  (22 Feb. 1984 –)

Elijah Stokes

Tre'Veon

Charmaine

Donald, Dennis
Sharneise, Charquita, Chardanae
Storee

Sharneise Stokes just graduated from East English Village High School and will be attending Western Michigan University in the fall of 2014.

Nathaniel and Zynquwandria   LuQuinda   Charquita

6. Victor Kevin Stokes
   (6 July 1963 – 28 Nov. 2013)

Mother Bette Dollison
Victor Dollison
(24 June 19?? –)
Victoria Dollison

Victor Stokes   Vic Dollison and son

Victoria and family

Mother Cherise Bridges

| Victor Kevin Stokes cont. . . | Kanisha Stokes
(13 Mar. 1986 -)
 -m- Christopher Robinson Sr.
(16 Oct. 1986 –) | Christopher Robinson Jr.
(4 Apr. 2003 –)
Kayla Robinson
(4 June 2006 –)
Kaliyah Robinson
(5 Feb. 2011 –) |

Kanisha

Kayla

Christopher

Cherise Bridges

Kaliyah

Kanisha and Christopher

ERNEST STOKES, SPOUSE – RUTH MADORA SHANNON

7. Elona Moore   Nai'lah Shabazz   Ansar Sakin
    (22 Apr. 1956 –)   Nai'lah Sakin

Elona Moore

Young Nai'lah, Nai'lah Sakin, Ansar

7
CHALMERS STOKES

CHALMERS STOKES, SPOUSE – LINDORA JOHNSON
(4 Dec. 1925 – 15 Aug. 1973)

Children

Frank E. Poole

(23 Feb. 1947 – 19??)

Shari Louise Stokes

(1 Jan. 1955 –)

-m- Willie Smith Jr.

Grand Children

Willie Smith III

(22 Dec. 1974 –)

 -m- Crystal

Aaron Charles Smith

(10 Nov. 1980 –)

Shari Smith

Willie and Crystal renewing their vows with family

Children of Chalmers Stokes and Mary Helen

Mary Helen Stokes (no other information available at this time)

8
CLARENCE STOKES

CLARENCE WILLIAM STOKES, SPOUSE – LILY MAY WILEY

Clarence Stokes was also married to a woman named Vickie. Two of Vickie's sisters was married to other Stokes brothers at one time or another. Sister Mary was married to Andrew, and sister Dolly was married to Marcellus. Dolly's youngest sister, Henrietta Patton was said to be "about the best aunt we ever had" according to many in the family who knew her.

Children	**Grandchildren**	**Great Grandchildren**
Clara Stokes		
Clarence William Stokes Jr. (17 May 1950 –)	Clarence William Stokes III (1975 –)	
Calvin Stokes (31 July 1951 –) -m- Mary Lee Green (16 Oct. 1945 –)	Sherry Denise Green (8 Aug. 1957 – Mar. 2000)	Kandia Denise Green Kimberly Green Nicolette Green Brian Green (23 Feb. 1985 –)
	Charisse Brown (18 Sep. 1968 –)	DeJuan Pettis (8 Dec. 1990 –) DeShawn Brown (7 July 1992 –)
	Valonda Green (24 Dec. 1969 –)	Bruce Hudson (5 Dec. 1986 –) Antonio Green (5 July 1988 –)
	Rochelle Louise Green (23 Mar. 1971 –)	
	Antoinette Marie Stokes (2 Apr. 1975 –)	

Bertha Lee Stokes
 (10 Oct. 1952 –)

Devlon Stokes
 (10 Feb. 1971 –)
Dequette Stokes
 (17 Jan. 1972 –)

Mary Joyce Stokes
 (5 June 1954 – 31 Jan. 2006)

Adelena Stokes
 (23 Apr. 1970 –)
Evelyn Stokes
 (26 Dec. 1971 –)
Shanessa Stokes
 (23 Sep. 1975 –)

JAMES STOKES

Children

Charles Blue   (No other information has been gathered about James Stokes at this time.)

9

MARCELLUS STOKES

Marcellus Stokes, spouse Naomi Yancey
(23 Mar. 1928 – 23 Feb. 2009)   (30 Mar. 1929 – 20 Oct. 1974)

Children	Grand Children	Great Grand Children
1. Marcellus "Mark" Stokes (28 Apr. 1948 – 8 Dec. 1998)		
2. Robert Anthony Stokes Sr. (13 June 1949 –) -m- Jessica Marie Ruffin (31 Oct. 1953 – May 2012	Anitha Janise Lamonica Stokes (7 May 1972 –) Robert Anthony Stokes Jr. (1 Jan. 1974 – 25 Oct. 2003) Lonnay Teaon Stokes (14 Oct. 1980 –) Lanita Stokes (9 Aug. 1984 –) Robneyon Currius Stokes (24 Oct. 1996 –)	

Jessica and Robert Stokes

Anitha Stokes

Robert Anthony Stokes Jr.

3. Brenda Stokes
   (22 Nov. 1951 –)

Sabrina Marie Stokes
  (28 Mar. 1967 –)
Rosetta Ann Stokes
  (4 Aug. 1969 –)
Clifford Aundra King II
  (27 Feb. 1971 –)
Lakissha Aundrea King
  (1 June 1973 –)

Brenda Stokes attended nursing school and worked as a nurse assistant supervisor. She also worked as a bus driver in Houston, Texas. She returned to Detroit in 1982 and began working for the City of Detroit for 25 years before retiring.

4. Ronald Stokes
   (9 June 1953 – 15 Feb. 2009)

Carolyn Scarborough

5. Kenneth William Stokes Sr.
   (16 Aug. 1954 –)

Mother is Barbara West
Kenneth William Stokes Jr.
  (5 Dec. 1972 –)
Naomi Marie Stokes
  (21 May 1974 –)

Kenneth William Stokes Jr.
  (21 Deb. 1973 –)
Jasmine Ilene Stokes
  (19 May 1975 –)

Kenneth Stokes Sr.

Mother is Regina Sheppard
Angela Stokes
 (12 Feb. 1985 –)
Jen Neta' Stokes
 (17 Feb. 1986 –)
Jeremiah James Stokes
 (22 Feb. 1990 –)

6. Ilene Marie Stokes
   (31 May 1956 –)
   -m- Lawrence Joseph Radford Sr.
   (4 Mar. 1955 –)

Lawrence Joseph Radford Jr.
(4 June 1973 –)
 -m- Julianna Radford

Ilene Radford

Lawrence and Ilene Radford

Lawrence and Julianna

Ilene Radford

Ilene Radford graduated from Indiana Wesleyan University with an Associates of Science degree in business on December 17, 2005 and a Bachelor of Science degree in Management on August 11, 2007. She earned a Master of Science degree with a major in Management on August 8, 2009. She obtained high recognition while pursuing her education as an honor student in her Master's program, Cum Laude in her bachelor's program, and Outstanding Student and Class Representative during her Associate's degree program.

Ilene has worked 25 years in the banking industry and 15 years in the health industry. She is currently working in the health industry as a manager.

		Mother is Tina Sanverivi
7. Valerie Jewel Stokes	JoAl Marcellus West	Elijah Joel West
(21 Feb. 1960 –)	(12 Sep. 1980 –)	(24 Nov. 2009 –)
-m- Jonathan Charles West	Tina Jewel Juliette West	Isaiah Antoine Washington
(15 Aug. 1954 –)	(13 May 1983 –)	(9 June 2003 –)
	-m- Andrè Rashaun Woods	Juliette Jewel Woods
	(30 Dec. 1977 –)	(11 Oct. 2007 –)

Valerie West worked 20 years in the banking industry and seven years in government before accepting her call to the ministry in 2000. She later received her bachelor's degree in business from Cornerstone University. In May 2012, Valerie earned her Master's of Divinity from Saint Paul School of Theology.

JoAl West earned his Bachelor's degree in Liberal Arts from Kentucky State University in 2005. In 2007 he joined the navy where he served four years and received an honorable discharge. He graduated from the University of Washington with a Master of Education in the Intercollegiate Athletic Leadership Program. He currently works at Standard Technology as a Navy Clinical Information Systems Trainer in San Diego,   California.

Tina Woods graduated from Jackson State University in Jackson, Mississippi with a bachelor's degree in psychology in 2006. She is currently enrolled in Oakland County Community College Nursing Program.

JoAl West, Tina Sanverivi, and Elijah West

8. James Daniel Stokes
   (30 June 1963 –)
   -m- Michelle Renee Hicks
   (23 Dec. 1970 –)

Jamez Daniel Stokes *mother is Rita Taylor*
 (4 Apr. 1986 –)
Cortez Alexander Stokes *mother is Rita Taylor*
 (12 Jan. 1988 –)

James Lamar Stokes
 (17 Nov. 1993 –)

James "BeBe" and Michelle

Jamez, Cortez, James Daniel, and James Lamar

10
MARCELLARS MOORE JR.

MARCELLARS MOORE JR., SPOUSE – LILLIE SHINE
(1897 – 19??)   (1905 – 19??)

Children   **Grandchildren**

1. Celeste Moore

2. Anna Mae Moore   Sonia Bingham
 -m- George Bingham Sr.   George Bingham Jr.
3. Mattie Moore   Clydee Bell Atkins
 (24 May 1926 – 28 July 1992)   (1946 – Sep. 2013)
   -m- Walter Atkins   Arnold Gene Atkins
                                 (1960 – July 2012)
                                Alfred Atkins
                                Pamela Atkins
                                David Atkins

Mattie Atkins

4. Colleen Marie Moore   Frank Stamps
     (15 Sep, 1927 – 22 May 2009)
     -m- Vernon Stamps
     (17 June 1936 – 17 Nov. 2013)

Colleen Stamps (left)

Walter Atkins (right)

unk, **Colleen Stamps**, unk, **Marcellars** (b.1897), **M.C.** (b. 1930)

Children	**Grand Children**	**Gr Grandchildren**	**Gr Gr Grandchildren** **GrGrGr Grand**
5. David Moore died at age 3			
6. Marcellars Charles Moore (25 Dec. 1930 –) "MC" -m- Rita Janet Francis (21 Aug. 1942 –)	*Mother is Lorain* 1. Gwendolyn Moore -m- Edward Eaves (10 Jan. 1940 –27 Mar. 2008)	Hollie Moore (28 Dec. 1972 –) -m- Joseph Nunn (16 Jan. 1973 –)	Antoine Swift (6 Apr. 1992 -)
		Shealtiel Nichole Moore (7 Nov. 1974 –)	
		Phanà Moore (11 May 1980 –) -m- Cortez McKay Sr.	Jasmine Bradford Morgan Davis DionAndrè Monet Cortez McKay Jr. Joshua Moore Gabrielle McKaya

Shealtiel Nichole Moore

Gwendolyn Eaves retired from Detroit Medical Center after 25 years of service. While there she worked as a unit clerk and was a union steward for many years. Mother of three, Gwen loves to travel, watch movies, and cook.

Jasmine, Gwendolyn, Hollie

Hollie and Joseph Nunn

Hollie Nunn Works at Macomb Community College as an audio visiual technician. She graduated from Oakland University in 2010 with a Bachelor's degree in Sociology. She plans to move to Florida in the near future and attend graduate school.

Joseph Nunn works at Aero Communications Corporation as a cable installer. Some of his favorite hobbies include gardening, watching basketball games and movies.

Cortez MacKay

Antoine Swift

Antoine Swift is a 2010 graduate of Chippewa High School. While in high school he played football, swam, and played the baritone in the band. He attends Oakland Community College majoring in accounting. He works as a swim instructor at Aqua Tots.

Jasmine and Phanà

Jasmine and Morgan

Jasmine Bradford says, "As childhood ends and adulthood begins, I realize that my years of dependency are wrapping up. At Cass Technical High School, I studied, volunteered, and participated in extracurricular activities. I was eager to learn, especially in my business courses. I brought in high grades, eagerly wrote short stories, participated in BPA contests, volunteered at school and in the community, went to Distributive Education Clubs of America (DECA) meetings, and critically thought about ideas and events. Although, I have been accepted to numerous colleges and Universities nationwide I am not committed to any school. My top choices are Wayne State University and University of Michigan-Dearborn."

Joshua

Gabrielle

Cortez Jr

Marcellus and Rita Moore cont . . .

Children	Grandchildren	Gr Grandchildren
Mother is Loretta 2. Sharon Jackson		
Mother is Maxine 3. Darren Moore	Tanya Moore	Tyler Mitchell Trevon Thomas

Meland Lerel Davis

	Grandchildren	
	Meland Lerel Davis (8 Mar. 1979 – 24 April 1974)	

Children	Grandchildren	Gr Grandchildren
4. Tina Moore -m- Milton Doyle	Brittani Buford Milton Doyle Jr.	
5. Byron Moore		
6. Charlotte Moore	Kathon Moore	Kathon Moore Jr. Kalia Moore Kalisa Moore Kathon Terrell Moore
	Arika Moore Sierra Moore	

7. Annette Moore
  -m- Steve Edwards
	Cliffton Moore
	Cortez Rackley
	  -m- Jasmine Rackley
	Steven Edwards	

Marcellus and Rita Moore cont . . .

	Children	Grandchildren	Gr Grandchildren
	Mother is Rita Moore		
	Yvette Baxter	Necia Baxter	
	Yolanda Baxter	Darien Baxter	
	Donna Baxter	Brandon Chatman	
	-m-David Daoud		
7. Frederick Marcellus Moore -m- Gwendolyn	Frederick Moore Jr.		
	mother is Mary Perry		
	Larry MacIntosh		
	Diane Perry		
	Shirley McFerren		

Frederick Marcellus Moore

10
RALEIGH MOORE

RALEIGH MOORE, SPOUSE – WINNIE PAYNE
(21 Feb. 1883 – 19??)   (6 June 1896 – 19??)

Children	Grandchildren	Great Grandchildren
Edward "E.C." Moore (12 Oct. 1919 -)	David Moore Leslie Moore Linda Moore	
Theary Moore Sr. (12 June 1920 – 26 Nov. 2011)	Theary Moore Jr. Linda Moore	
Orange W. Moore (13 Mar. 1922 – 8 July 1994) -m- Shellie	Orlanda Moore Sandra Moore	
Raleigh "R.L." Moore (25 Nov. 1923 – 1 Nov. 2000)		
Overzina Moore (22 Nov. 1925 -) -m- Lorenzo Ross (?? – Feb. 1995)	Ronald Ross Lorraine Ross Paul Ross	Tori Ross Finnegan Joey Ross -m Sean Ray Michael Ross Kelly Orange
	Barbara Ross Jesse Ross James Ross	

MORE FAMILY PHOTOS

Chalmers Samuel Stokes   Andrew Stokes   Ernest Severe Stokes

Ethel and Cynthia in restaurant owned by Ethel located in Detroit's historical Black Bottom.

Adelina, Lindora, Sister Robertson from church, Ethel and Dolly

Aunt Cora used to live in a bus in Illinois. She was later brought to Michigan to live with Andrew Stokes.

Mark, Ethel, Andrew, Brenda, and Dolly

This is the 1870 United States Census. It shows John Stokes, age 26, already grown with a family of his own living right next door to his parents, Henry, 58 and Rioriah Stokes, 48. He is married to Nellie, age 23, with two children, Annie and Johnnie ages four and one respectively.

The 1880 Census shows John and Nellie 40 and 30 respectively with seven children: Anna, John, Betty, Nella, William, Manthews, and Laura. These children range in age from 14 to two years old. John is listed as a farmer. His wife, Nellie, is listed as "keeping house."

Unfortunately much of the 1890 U.S. Census was destroyed, so I am unable to get a picture of it.

In the U.S 1900 Census, John is now listed as 56 and his Nellie is 50. With discrepancies found in at least two of the records, John could have been born any time between 1840 and 1844 and Nellie between 1847 and 1850. There are also five grandchildren living with them ranging from ages 15 to two. Could it be that one or more of John and Nellie's older children died and left five orphans? Or were they just absent from the home for one reason or another? In any case, this is a prime example of how we pull together as a family in times of need.

Have we now found Nellie's maiden name? John's mother-in-law, Pollie Wilson lives with them also. She was born in Virginia around 1830. Pollie had given birth to eight children, but only four were living at the time the 1900 census was taken. Was Nellie born as Nellie Wilson? Or had her mother remarried?

We also see Daniel listed as a son for the first time. He is now 16 years old born in November 1883 in Mississippi. This is the same Daniel who later grows up to marry Adelina Moore.

This is where we see MC and Ella Moore with two of their three children. The third child, Altha is on the next page of the same census record. Also, we see much of the Stokes family living on the same street in several different households.

This 1850 Census shows Mary Jane Tyler at age 4. This is the Mary who later grows up to marry Joe Moore and became our own Mary Tyler Moore. Her father is listed as what looks like Daniel or David Tyler born in South Carolina. Later census records show the spelling to be Derrill Tyler. Her mother's name is Martha born in Alabama.

Dwelling-houses numbered in the order of visitation	Families numbered in the order of visitation	The name of every person whose usual place of abode on the first day of June, 1860, was in this family.	Description.			Profession, Occupation, or Trade of each person, male and female, over 15 years of age.	Value of Estate Owned.		Place of Birth, Naming the State, Territory, or Country.	Married within the year	Attended school within the year	Persons over 20 yr's of age who cannot read & write	Whether deaf and dumb, blind, insane, idiotic, pauper, or convict.	
			Age.	Sex.	White, Black, or mulatto		Value of Real Estate.	Value of Personal Estate.						
1	2	3	4	5	6	7	8	9	10	11	12	13	14	
		Joseph Cole	3	m					Texas			1		1
		Matilda Finley	17	f					Mississippi					2
262	370	John W. Wright	29	m		Farmer		112	Alabama	1				3
		Tolitha "	30	f					"		1			4
		Martha "	7	f					Texas			2		5
		John H "	12	m					"		1			6
263	371	Joseph Coody	47	m		Farmer	640	355	Tennessee	1	1			7
		Hester "	45	f					Texas			2		8
		Frank "	16	m					Louisiana	1				9
		Barbara C "	11	f					Texas			2		10
264	372	Derrill Tyler	42	m		Farmer	4350	12416	S Carolina	1				11
		Mary J "	15	f					Miss	1				12
		Martha "	23	f					Ala	1				13
		Abner E "	12	m					Miss	1				14
		Wm D "	11	m					"					15
		H A "	7	m					Texas			1		16
		George W "	5	m					"			1		17
		Columbus "	4	m					"			1		18
		La Fayette "	12/12	m					"			1		19
		Elisha T Edwards	17	m		Farm Hand			Miss	1				20
		Lucinda M "	14	f			2000	4600	"		4			21
		Virginia R "	12	f					"		1			22
		Henrietta R "	10	f					"		1			23
265	373	Wm Berry	50	m		Physician	800	2062	England	1				24
		Henrietta "	30	f					Alabama	1				25
		Nancy "	8	f					Texas			2		26
		Sarah "	6	f					"			2		27
		Frances "	1	f					"			2		28
266	374	Joseph Pattenkite	35	m		Farmer	12000	28000	Georgia	1				29
267	375	Jesse B Evans	40	m		"	17030	11305						30
		Lucretia "	22	f					Texas			2		31
		Martha "	2	f					"			2		32
		Edward "	1	m					"			1		33
268	376	Sarah Evans	79	f			5600	15300	N Carolina					34
269	377	Thos Evans	55	m		Farmer	900	4786	" "	1				35
		Lucretia C "	37	f					Va				+	36
		Wm H "	19	m		Farm Hand			Ala	1				37
		Sarah E "	16	f					"	1				38
		Thos T "	12	m					"	1				39
														40
No. white males, 20 No. colored males, _____ No. foreign born, _____ No. blind, _____	No. white females, 19 No. colored females, _____ No. deaf and dumb, _____ No. insane, _____						43940	79746	No. idiotic, _____ No. pauper, _____				No. convicts, _____	

In the 1860 census Mary Jane Tyler's father is more clearly written as Derrill Tyler. I must admit that this part of the research was gathered by someone else. I have not yet verified that the Mary Jane Tyler found on these last two census records are indeed the same Mary Tyler who married Joe Moore. The research has just begun!

ABOUT THE AUTHOR

Bonita Stokes Walker grew up on the west side of Detroit, Michigan. She studied journalism at Wayne State University and graduated in 1985 with a Bachelors of Arts degree. Instead of going into journalism, she worked as a customer service representative for Michigan Bell Telephone Company which later became Ameritech. While there, she began taking classes for her next career – teaching. She received her Master of Arts degree in Elementary Education in 1995 also from Wayne State University. She taught in both public schools and charter schools in Detroit, Michigan and Sacramento, California, finally retiring in June 2013.

Genealogy has been a passion for her since her early years when she heard both her grandmother and mother refer to a cousin as "Cousin Na" short for Cousin Naomi. How can this lady be both her grandmother's cousin and her mother's cousin at the same time? How could she be Bonita's cousin? Even after her first family reunion on her mother's side of the family in 1987 Bonita left more confused than ever. The family reunion name was called Marshall Buckner Mayberry Reunion. A Mayberry descendant, she began meeting family members named Marshall and Buckner. How could that be? Who are these people she was supposed to be kin to? That's when her real research began. She started by talking to relatives and getting to know them. She joined Ancestry.com and began her internet search to find answers to her perplexing questions. And find them, she did.

Her research took her as far back as 1801 on her mother's side, and mid-1800s on her father's side. DNA results show that her maternal line hailed from Sierra Leone, Africa. When she began her research on her maternal ancestors, she knew she had to share this information in writing. She also knew that someone, anyone had to begin recording our history as we are currently making it so that future generations won't be so stumped and unable to research beyond three or four generations. So Family Ties was created. First, with the help of family she compiled Marshall Buckner Mayberry Family Ties in 1998 denoting her maternal ancestors. It was completely revamped into a 100 page full color book in 2004. It wasn't until 2014 that Ross Moore Stokes Family Ties came into existence with a lot of help from family members.

After spending ten years in Sacramento, California, Bonita relocated back to her home town where she enjoys genealogy research and traveling. She promotes her travel business through network marketing. Bonita currently resides in Warren, Michigan. She has two daughters and one grandson. Follow her on Facebook, Twitter, and Instagram.

Websites:	www.BonitaWalker.com
	www.MarshallBucknerMayberry.com
	www.RossMooreStokes.webs.com
	www.BonitaWalker.WorldVenvtures.biz
Facebook:	Bonita Stokes Walker
Twitter:	@IamBonitaWalker
Instagram:	@IamBonitaWalker
Email:	WalkerBRW@aol.com

www.ingramcontent.com/pod-product-compliance
Lightning Source LLC
Chambersburg PA
CBHW041508280526
45792CB00004B/1171